Return to the Father

Eight services of reconciliation
for the Catholic secondary school

Tony Castle

Kevin Mayhew

First published in 2000 by
KEVIN MAYHEW LTD
Buxhall
Stowmarket
Suffolk IP14 3BW

ISBN 1 84003 508 0
Catalogue No. 1500337

Cover design by Jonathan Stroulger
Edited by Helen Elliot
Typesetting by Louise Selfe
Printed in Great Britain

Dedicated to
Father Roger Barralet OFM
in gratitude and friendship

Contents

Introduction 7

Order of Service 1
- **The Little Man in the Tree** 11
- Examination of Conscience 14

Order of Service 2
- **The Hairy Prophet** 17
- Examination of Conscience 21

Order of Service 3
- **The Unforgiving Servant** 23
- Examination of Conscience 27

Order of Service 4
- **Return to the Father** 29
- Examination of Conscience 33

Order of Service 5
- **The King Who Sinned** 35
- Examination of Conscience 40

Order of Service 6
- **The Weeping Sinner** 43
- Examination of Conscience 46

Order of Service 7
- **The Condemned Woman** 49
- Examination of Conscience 52

Order of Service 8
- **Peter Disowns Jesus** 55
- Examination of Conscience 59

The Order of Service sheet 61

Suggested readings for Services of Reconciliation 63

Introduction

Every Christian community has the duty, and also the challenge, of providing its members with the opportunity for reconciliation with God and one another. Every Eucharist, for example, opens with a simple penitential rite, and later comes the sign of peace.

As Christian communities, our schools have such a duty to their members; the challenge is not always easily met. The eight services that follow are the fruit and culmination of strenuous and painstaking efforts to meet this challenge, and have proved to be very successful. Some of the plays and examinations of conscience have also been adapted for use in parish settings, where they have been well received.

Naturally, every school has to work out for itself how best to provide the time and place for a service, or services, of reconciliation, according to its own particular circumstances; and how that service will relate to the actual Sacrament of Reconciliation. The following description of the practice of one secondary school, from which these services come, may suggest ideas to others.

Sharing good liturgical practice

The school in question does not have a hall large enough to accommodate the whole student body of Years 7 to 13 (approximately 780). However the local parish church, which will seat half of the school, is just next door, quietly removed from the bustle of school life. The services of reconciliation are always conducted in the parish church.

The whole school community attends a service of reconciliation during Advent, towards the end of term, and during Lent. In order to make the numbers manageable the service is repeated three times, once for each age group. For example, in Advent, Years 7 and 9 have theirs on a Wednesday morning in mid-December; Years 8 and 10 on the following Friday morning and Years 11, 12 and 13 on the last Wednesday, just before breaking up for Christmas.

The liturgy in detail

The liturgy falls into two related parts. The service of reconciliation, which all attend, takes about twenty minutes. As it concludes everyone is invited to stay to see one of the priests for the Sacrament of Reconciliation. On average (it varies from Year to Year; with Year 7 being enthusiastic and Years 12 and 13 reluctant!) 70 students per service, and the occasional member of staff, stay for confession. Those who leave the church return to lessons. The school chaplains (each Year has its own) and other priests from the local deanery are invited to lead the services and be available afterwards for the sacrament. Three or four priests are required for each service.

Since the time that all this will take cannot be accurately predicted, it was decided to have the services in the hour period before lunch, so that some of lunch-time can be used if, as is usually the case, the priests need the time to see all the penitents. (Recently a group of Year 7 pupils waited quietly and patiently in the church for over an hour before seeing a priest.) One of the priests uses the confessional room, where there is the option of not being seen (very popular with many pupils!) The other priests are given sites in the side chapels or the sacristy.

The biggest worry the students have is, 'What do I say to the priest?' The Order of Service sheet should carry clear and simple directions for the pupils to follow as they prepare for the Sacrament of Reconciliation (see page 62). It is important not to neglect this provision because students are often willing to approach the sacrament but do not do so because of either peer pressure or the simple fear of not knowing what to do. While the former is difficult to combat (an appeal to 'think for yourself and don't blindly follow others' could be made at the end of the service), the latter can and should be provided for.

Leadership of the service

A service of reconciliation does *not* have to be followed by the Sacrament of Reconciliation. The services are complete and free-standing without the Sacrament being offered afterwards. If a service is being used in this way it is not necessary to have a priest present. The service can be led by a member of staff or any approved lay person. The introduction provides an opportunity for the leader to tie the service in to the Advent or Lent season, as appropriate.

If a priest is presiding, it is still a good idea to have a confident member of staff at the microphone to introduce the hymns, the drama and so on.

Order of service

A specially printed service sheet is essential. Presumably the school, or the parish church, will have hymn books so there is no need to go to the trouble and expense of printing out the words of the hymns (if you reproduce copyright material you will have to seek clearance and pay a charge). A model of a suggested Order of Service sheet will be found on pages 61 and 62.

Readings or dramas

The school drama department, if given sufficient time to plan, may be very willing to produce the play chosen for the service. The scripts offered in this book can, of course, be altered, adapted or improved upon.

If it is not possible to use a play then the Scripture reading from which the play is taken, or one from the list provided (see page 63) can be used or perhaps adapted for reading in parts. The liturgy of the word, whether it is performed as a play or read as a straight text, should be well rehearsed.

The examination of conscience

Each play has its own examination of conscience. The celebrant, or service leader, should introduce this and then leave the reading to two students, each with a microphone or sharing one. *It is essential that this is well rehearsed.* The two readers must understand what they are doing; they are not simply reading a text, like a passage from the Bible. They are leading a meditation, a stimulus to thought. After each sentence, or phrase, there must be a silence, a time for reflection. There should also be a long reflective pause between each reader.

The adolescent readers should be allowed, perhaps encouraged, to adapt the wording if, in their judgement, it is not expressing an idea or thought in the language of the teenage listeners, though some guidance may be necessary here.

The prayer of contrition

This is the centre and purpose of the whole service. This is the response to the stimulus of, first, the biblical drama and then the examination of conscience. It does not have to be long or complex. Most priests are happy to use one or two of the prayers on the back of the service sheet (see page 61). If a fuller prayer of contrition is desired, there is the 'I confess' which is often used at Mass. It is important that the words of the prayer are available to the students so that they all have the opportunity to join in. This, and the subsequent opportunity to stay for the sacrament, is where the students' freedom to join in or not must be respected.

Recipients of the sacrament

Moslem, Hindu and Sikh girls (the school concerned is a Catholic High School for girls) have often asked if they too could stay behind after the service and go to speak to one of the priests. With the full approval of the clergy, *all* the students are told at the commencement of the service that anyone who wishes to may approach one of the confessors. But, and this is made very clear, if the student is not a Catholic she must say to the priest, 'I'm not a Catholic but I would like to speak to you'.

It sets a wonderful example if some of the staff are seen staying behind and quietly going to the sacrament.

The hymns

All the fully worked out services provided have actually been used, some several times, and the hymns shown are those which the pupils of this particular school know. Any other school using these services needs to be confident that the students are familiar with the hymns chosen, or else select others. A service of reconciliation is not the time or place for experimentation with new hymns. The atmosphere should be 'up-beat' and confident. The same applies to the drama. It is better not to attempt the use of drama unless the performance is confident and assured.

The hymn suggestions can be found in *Hymns Old and New,* New Century Edition (HON), *Liturgical Hymns Old and New* (LITON) or *Praying in Song* (PS), the hymnbook for Catholic secondary schools, all published by Kevin Mayhew Ltd.

The word 'reconciliation'

This word is not in common use among pupils and needs 'unwrapping' for them. They are all familiar with the idea of 'making up', when problems between friends and in friendship groups need sorting out. It might, therefore, mean more to pupils to refer to the service, and the sacrament, as 'Making-up time': making up with God and with one another.

Order of Service 1

Opening hymn — *Come, Lord Jesus, come* — HON 95, verses 1, 5 & 6
LITON 214
PS 116

Introduction — Why we are gathered.

Prayer

Heavenly Father,
at this time of the year
we look for the coming of our Lord, Jesus Christ.
We want to prepare well for our celebration of his birth;
may we use this opportunity
to make our hearts and minds ready,
so that, reconciled to you and to one another,
we may fittingly celebrate your Son's appearing among us.
Amen.

Drama — *Little Man in the Tree*

Hymn — *Walk with me, O my Lord* — HON 441
LITON 706
PS 371

Examination of conscience

Prayer(s) of contrition (sorrow for sin) — See prayers 1 or 2 on back of sheet
(Read together)

Hymn — *Sing it in the valleys* — LITON 619
PS 322

Invitation — If you would like to receive the sacrament of God's forgiveness, please stay behind now to meet with one of the priests.

The Little Man in the Tree

Luke 19:1-10

Preparations If the Art Department can help, a coloured cut-out of a large tree, with step ladder out of sight behind it, would be invaluable. It should be placed left of centre-stage.

Characters A narrator, Jesus, Peter, Zacchaeus (has to be a small student), three people in the crowd, a crowd (preferably tall pupils).

(The narrator needs to stand a little apart from the action, if possible at a microphone.)

Narrator Our story takes place in the ancient city of Jericho, which is in the great rift valley that separates the countries of modern Israel and Jordan. *(Aside)* If you look up Jericho in the *Guinness Book of Records* you will find that it is the oldest city in the world.

At the time of Jesus, Jericho was a busy place with many shops and crowds of people. It also had a number of tax collectors *(crowd boo)* who worked for the hated Romans *(crowd boo).* The tax collectors were very unpopular because they cheated people. The chief tax collector in the Jericho area was a short, boring-looking man called Zacchaeus. Here he comes now . . .

(Enter Zacchaeus left. The crowd is drifting into view right.)

Person 1 *(Pointing)* Watch out, everyone, here comes that rat, Zacchaeus.

(Crowd look and pass comments to one another.)

Person 2 *(Suddenly noticing Jesus approaching with his followers)* Never mind him *(pointing),* here comes Jesus, the prophet from Nazareth.

(Jesus enters right. People crowd around Jesus; Zacchaeus is ignored.)

Peter Stop pushing! Give Jesus some room, please.

Person 3 Are you going to speak to us, Jesus?

Person 2 Are you going to tell one of your stories?

(Zacchaeus joins the back of the crowd, but cannot see.)

Person 1 Master, can you give me some advice?

Person 3 Can you pray for my uncle Ben, he's very ill?

Peter *(Insistently)* Will you please make way?

(Zacchaeus gives up trying to see, runs ahead and 'climbs' the tree.)

Jesus Yes, I'll pray for your uncle. Why don't you pray? God is our loving Father. If you ask, he will hear you.

Peter *(Loud and insistent) Please* stop pushing.

Jesus *(Speaking to Person 1)* What advice did you want?

Person 1 Rabbi, there's a man here in Jericho who is spreading lies about me. What should I do?

Jesus You start by forgiving him.

(Zacchaeus is listening from the tree. Suddenly Jesus notices him.)

Jesus Come down from up there, Zacchaeus. Hurry. I would like you to invite me to dinner tonight.

(There's an immediate silence in the crowd.)

Peter *(Horrified)* You can't do that, Master. You can't go with him, he's a terrible sinner . . . he's a tax collector!

Jesus I know who he is and what he does.

Person 1 You must be mad! No decent Jew mixes and eats with the likes of him.

Person 3 Don't you understand? He's a sinner.

Person 2 This is out of order. Disgusting! I'm going home.

(Departs. Others leave as well.)

Peter *(Addressing Jesus)* Can't you see . . . if you mix with these low-lives the decent Jews will leave you.

Zacchaeus *(Speaking to Jesus)* Master, I'm sorry for what I've done. I really want to make a fresh start. I'll not cheat people ever again. I'll pay back everything I've taken – I'll repay every penny. I'll sell my big house and give the money to the poor.

Jesus Well done, Zacchaeus. *(Speaking to the crowd)* You see, everyone, God loves the sinner who says sorry. Understand, I've come to seek out and save those who have lost their way.

(Crowd drift off to the right . . . Jesus, Zacchaeus, Peter and the others go off to the left.)

Examination of Conscience

following the play *The Little Man in the Tree*

Celebrant/service leader

We have just seen and enjoyed the story of Zacchaeus, the tax-collector who wanted to see Jesus. Zacchaeus got much more than he had expected; an opportunity to obtain forgiveness and a real relationship with Jesus. Let us look more carefully at the story to see if we can apply what happened to Zacchaeus to our own relationships.

Reader A

Let us think about the play from the Gospels which we have just seen. Let us see if it applies to our relationship with Jesus, our Lord.

Pause

Reader B

We are going to think about the ways in which we fail, the things we do wrong; so that we can use today's opportunity to say 'sorry' and build anew our relationship with Jesus.

Pause

Reader A

Zacchaeus desperately wanted to see Jesus. How keen are we to keep our friendship with Jesus alive? Do we talk to God or Jesus in prayer? Do we meet Christ and his other friends at Mass on Sundays?

Pause

Reader B

The crowd turned their backs on Zacchaeus. Do we deliberately turn our backs on anyone? Do we shut out any other girl or boy from our group? Do we hurt others by spreading stories about them? Do we make fun of any girl or boy?

Pause

Reader A

'I would like you to invite me to dinner,' Jesus says to Zacchaeus. How are you with your friends? Are you a loyal and good friend? How are you with your brothers and sisters? Are you ever mean or spiteful? Do you behave with dignity and respect for yourself when you are out with others?

Pause

Reader B

Some of the crowd wandered off and left Jesus. Are you stuck up or snobbish, thinking yourself better than others? Do you judge other people without knowing the facts? Do you try to get on with everyone?

Pause

Reader A

Zacchaeus was sorry for cheating people. Do you ever cheat? Have you taken money, or things that don't belong to you? Do you tell lies? Do you try to make up with people when you know you have been in the wrong?

Pause

Reader B

Zacchaeus says, 'I will give money to the poor.' Are you generous in helping the poor and the needy? Or are you selfish, only thinking of yourself? When you know someone is in trouble, do you offer help or duck out of the way?

Pause

Celebrant/service leader

Let's be quiet for a few moments, thinking of any other things we might have done, or failed to do; anything we might have done to damage our friendship with God and one another.

Order of Service 2

Opening hymn	*Do not be afraid*	HON 109, verses 1, 2 and 5 LITON 240 PS 129

Introduction

Why we are gathered.

Prayer

Almighty God,
before Jesus, your Son, came among us
to start his work of proclaiming the Good News,
you sent John the Baptist to prepare the way.
May we listen to his call to change our ways
and repent of the wrong we have done.
We ask this through Jesus Christ our Lord.
Amen.

Drama

The Hairy Prophet

Hymn	*How lovely on the mountains (Our God reigns)*	HON 182, verses 1, 3 and 4 LITON 346 PS 184

Examination of conscience

Prayer(s) of contrition (sorrow for sin)

See prayers 1 or 2 on back of sheet
(Read together)

Hymn	*Though the mountains may fall*	HON 426, verses 1, 2 and 4 LITON 688 PS 362

Invitation

If you would like to receive the sacrament of God's forgiveness, please stay behind now to meet with one of the priests.

THE HAIRY PROPHET

Luke 3:1-18 and Matthew 3:1-12

Preparations For John the Baptist, an old fur coat, half length or full, would be useful; a staff or long stick; a good flowing wig of dishevelled hair could be worn but it should not be comical. John is a figure of awe and power, not a clown. No one else should dress up.
For the sound man, a broom with a grey cloth over the brush.

Characters A radio presenter (rather brash); accompanying sound engineer (not a speaking part); Ben, the news reader; John the Baptist – the choice of 'John the Baptiser' is important. The role should be played by a strong, dominant character with a powerful voice; crowd of 8 to 10; three Pharisees; two soldiers; two tax collectors.

Radio presenter *(On microphone)* This is Beth Goldstein of Station RZ. Welcome to Radio Zion on this bright autumn morning. Right after the news I will be taking you on an outside broadcast, to the banks of the Jordan, where a new, rather hairy, prophet has appeared. A real Old Testament guy. Over now to Ben in the news-room.

Ben, newscaster Thank you, Beth. The headlines this morning: Pontius Pilate, the Roman governor, ordered a detachment of Roman soldiers to Tiberias, in Galilee, early this morning, where there have been more riots threatened. The increase in taxes to 45 per cent is causing nation-wide unrest.

Details are now available of yesterday's tower disaster at Siloam. 18 builders were killed and 26 seriously injured. The water supply to the south of Jerusalem will be restored later today.

That's all the news for the present. Our full news report can be heard at midday. I'm returning you now to Beth, and her exciting assignment down at the Jordan by Jericho. Is this new prophet the promised Messiah that everyone is looking for?

(The crowd come forward from the right, look round them, the radio presenter joins them.)

Radio presenter Well, thanks for the news, Ben. Now for our outside broadcast from the Jordan. I am standing in a large group of people on the banks of the Jordan; they have been here since dawn and we are looking out for the new prophet, John bar Zechariah. There's no sign of him yet . . . *(Looking round. At that moment John comes from the back of the audience/congregation.)*

John	*(Bellowing as he walks down the centre of the congregation)* Repent! Repent! You will all perish unless you repent. *(Repeat as necessary)*
Radio presenter	OK, listeners. I bet you can hear that all the way back to Jerusalem without your radio.
John	*(To the crowd)* Prepare the way of the Lord. Prepare, the Messiah is coming. Make the paths straight for his appearing. The mountains must be made low and the crooked roads smooth and straight. Prepare I say, prepare.
Radio presenter	*(Approaching John)* Excuse me, Sir, may I have a word?
	(Sound man holds the boom microphone towards John.)
John	A word, a word! You don't need a word. You need to stop all this flapping around and repent.
Radio presenter	*(Undisturbed)* Who and what are you, exactly, Sir?
John	I am a voice crying in the wilderness, 'Prepare the way of the Lord'.
Radio presenter	You are not the Messiah, then?
John	No, I am not even worthy to untie the strap of his sandals. I am the voice crying 'Prepare the way'!
Tax collectors	How shall we prepare?
John	You must be more honest and only collect the taxes you are required to. No more fiddling.
Soldiers	What should we do?
John	You must stop bullying people and extorting money from them. And stop grumbling about your pay.
Radio presenter	Excuse me, sir, I'm from Radio Zion. Our listeners are keen to know more about you and your message.
	(Sound man holds microphone towards John.)
John	Me? You do not need to know more about me; he who is to come, him you must listen to. He is from God. My message is, 'Repent, stop your sinning'.

Radio presenter Isn't that a bit, well, old fashioned?

John Do you want the Christ to come? *(Not waiting for an answer)* Do you want to be happy? What is old fashioned about wanting the Christ to come and hearing his message that will bring happiness? Repent! *(John moves away and returns the way he has come, through the centre of the congregation.)* Repent! Give up your wrong-doing. Prepare!

Radio presenter *(Into mike)* Well, there you have it. John has gone. It is said that he is getting the nickname 'Baptist' because he often plunges people who repent into the waters of the Jordan. We did not see that today; but we certainly heard his message! I'm returning you now to the studio. This is Beth Goldstein signing off until the same time tomorrow.

Examination of Conscience

following the play *The Hairy Prophet*

Celebrant/service leader

In the play we have just seen, John the Baptist, the hairy prophet, called on everyone to repent in preparation for the coming of Jesus, the Christ. As we prepare to celebrate how Christ came to us as a tiny baby, we too need to think of what we have done wrong, or failed to do, and repent.

Reader A

John cries out, 'Repent, repent!' To repent means to be really sorry for wrong-doing; having a change of heart about our behaviour. Do we take seriously the need we each have to struggle to be a better person? Do we say 'sorry' to God and apologise to the people we hurt when we do wrong? Or are we proud and unwilling even to consider that we sin?

Pause

Reader B

John says, 'You must be more honest.' Are we honest and to be trusted? Do we tell the truth or deceive people who trust us? Have you taken anything that doesn't belong to you? Have you returned CDs, books or anything else you have borrowed from friends? When your parents or guardians trust you, are you reliable or do you let them down?

Pause

Reader A

John says, 'You must stop bullying . . . and stop grumbling.' Do we ever hurt other people with violent actions or spiteful comments? Have you been mean to your brothers and sisters? Are you loving and kind to everyone in your form? Have you been a good and loyal friend? Do you take a negative attitude to life and keep grumbling about things?

Pause

Reader B

John asks, 'Do you want the Christ to come?' We want Christmas to come because of what we hope to get, but do we want Christ himself as our friend? Do we keep our relationship with God alive by talking to him in prayer? Do we meet with his friends on a Sunday at Mass? Will you celebrate Christmas by being at Mass on Christ's birthday?

Pause

Reader A

'Do you want to be happy?' Everyone wants to be happy; do we ruin anyone's happiness by our selfishness or thoughtlessness? Do we help at home, or do we leave all the jobs to our parents or guardians? Do we look out for anyone who is lonely and unhappy and offer them our friendship? Do we remember to be generous to the needy and poor?

Pause

Celebrant/service leader Let's sit quietly for a minute or two and think about what we have just been reminded of, and think of any other things we have done that we are sorry for.

Order of Service 3

Opening hymn	*Walk with me, O my Lord*	HON 441, verses 1-4 LITON 706 PS 371
Introduction	Why we are gathered.	
Prayer	Loving Father, you have assured us that each and every one of our sins will be forgiven; but there are two conditions. First, you expect us to be really and truly sorry for what we have done; and you want us to offer our forgiveness to those who have hurt us. Help us to be sincere in forgiving others and genuine in our efforts to be better Christians. Amen.	
Drama	*The Unforgiving Servant*	
Hymn	*God forgave my sin*	HON 145 LITON 286 PS 157
Examination of conscience		
Prayer(s) of contrition (sorrow for sin)	See prayers 1 or 2 on back of sheet *(Read together)*	
Hymn	*Make me a channel of your peace*	HON 262 LITON 470 PS 263
Invitation	If you would like to receive the sacrament of God's forgiveness, please stay behind now to meet with one of the priests.	

The Unforgiving Servant

Matthew 18:21-35

Preparations A 'throne' or imposing-looking chair required.

Characters Jesus; Peter; King; Clerk; Three guards (2 and 3 have no spoken parts); Unforgiving servant; Four other servants.

(Jesus and Peter walk on, talking quietly. They stop centre and Peter is now heard.)

Peter Yes, I know you have said it is very important to forgive; but it's hard. Anyway, what do you do if someone offends you again and again? Do you forgive them as many as seven times?

Jesus Oh, no, Peter, not seven times. *(Laughing)* More like seventy times seven times. Those who follow me, who want to be part of the Kingdom of God, must be generous in forgiving. It's rather like this . . . *(Peter and Jesus move off-stage and watch the proceedings as part of the audience. The throne is brought in and placed centre. The king enters and sits on the throne. A guard, who stands beside the king, follows him. Clerk enters and bows.)*

Clerk Your Majesty, I have been checking the annual accounts, as you ordered and find that one of your servants has not repaid the large loan you made him a year ago.

King *(To the guard)* Go and find this man and bring him to me. *(Addresses clerk as guard leaves)* Are the rest of my accounts in order?

Clerk Yes, Sire. There's a healthy profit this year.

(Two guards appear, half-dragging the servant.)

King Ah, here you are. Why have you avoided repaying my loan? How much do you owe me?

Unforgiving servant Much more than I can afford to repay, Your Highness.

King How much?

Unforgiving servant A hundred thousand pounds, Sire. Please have mercy . . . I have no way of repaying you. Think of my family who will be

	without food and clothing if you imprison me. Please, please have mercy.
King	I could sell you and your family as slaves. That would raise some of what you owe. Then I *could* let you off . . .
Unforgiving servant	*(Grovelling)* Please, Sire, please give me more time.
King	No . . . I will not give you more time. But as I'm feeling merciful today I will cancel all your debt. Go back to your family and don't get into debt again.
Unforgiving servant	Thank you, thank you, Sire. You are magnificent and generous. Thank you.
	(King, guards, clerk and throne all exit left. Servant wanders to the right for a moment. When area is clear he wanders back. Servant 2, speaking quietly to Servant 3, comes into view.)
Unforgiving servant	*(Arrogantly)* Oi, you! Yes, you! Come here a minute.
Servant 2	Me? Do you mean me?
Unforgiving servant	Yes, you. Where's my money? You owe me ten pounds.
	(Grabs hold of Servant 2 and forces him to the ground.)
Servant 2	Please give me time. I've not got ten pounds on me. I'll get it for you tomorrow.
Unforgiving servant	I want it now. Now, do you hear?
Servant 3	Leave him alone. Give him a bit of time.
Unforgiving servant	You keep out of this, or you'll be sorry! *(Sees a guard approaching)* Guard, here. Take this fellow off to prison. He owes me money.
	(All leave the stage area. Throne is returned to its place. King enters and sits. Guard either side. Servants 3, 4 and 5 enter, bow low.)
Servant 3	Your Highness, may we speak with you?
King	You may. What troubles you?
	(Approaching closer to the throne.)
Servant 3	Sire, you remember how this morning, in your great goodness

you forgave the debt of the servant who owed you a vast sum of money?

King Yes, I do.

Servant 4 Well, he has had one of our friends thrown into prison for owing him just ten pounds.

Servant 3 Yes, I was there and saw it all.

King *(Turning to the guards)* Go and get him. *(To the servants)* You did well to tell me of this. I shall see that this unforgiving servant is severely punished.

(Guards appear dragging a reluctant servant.)

King You evil man. I cancelled your huge debt to me because you begged and pleaded. Could you not have forgiven your fellow servant such a small sum, just as I forgave you? You are utterly evil. *(To the guards)* Arrest his wife and children and have them sold as slaves. This creature *(indicating the prone servant),* give him to the prison guards. He can stay in prison until the whole debt is repaid.

(All freeze. Jesus and Peter get up and half turn to face the audience.)

Jesus That is what your heavenly Father expects, Peter. We must all be generous in forgiving one another.

Examination of Conscience

following the play *The Unforgiving Servant*

Celebrant/service leader

The play we have just seen, based upon one of the stories Jesus told, really brings home the importance of being forgiving. We no longer have kings and courts like they did at the time of Jesus, but we still have debts and people who borrow money.

Reader A

Let us think about the meaning of the play based on the words of Jesus in Matthew's Gospel.

Reader B

Peter asks how many times he should forgive. How many times have we been forgiven by our parents and guardians for the bad things we have done? Are we grateful for their willing and ready forgiveness? Do we really respect them and appreciate all that they do for us? Are we grateful to God, our loving Father, for the many times in the past when he has forgiven us our sins?

Pause

Reader A

The servant avoids repaying his loan. Are we good at avoiding things? Do we try to avoid helping at home; making excuses instead of willingly giving a hand? Have we borrowed money from someone and not repaid it? Have we borrowed a CD or a book and not returned it?

Pause

Reader B

The king generously lets the servant off his debt. Are we generous with others, offering to help, showing them the love Jesus asks us to show? Are we generous with our money? Or are we mean and selfish, not ready and willing to share what we have? Do we help the poor and the needy?

Pause

Reader A

The unforgiving servant threatens his fellow servant. Do we ever use threatening words or actions? Are you guilty of bullying anyone? Do you say spiteful and mean things to your brothers or sisters? What are you like with your friends? Have you deliberately hurt anyone by what you've done or said? Have you spread stories about someone?

Pause

Reader B

The servants go and tell the king what has happened. Do you always tell the truth? Have we always been honest and open with our parents, our guardians and our teachers? Are we trustworthy? If you are in a post of responsibility, like a form captain or prefect, do you fulfil your jobs as well as you can?

Pause

Reader A

The king sends the unforgiving servant to prison. When we have done wrong do we make up excuses for our behaviour or honestly tell the truth and maturely accept whatever punishment is involved? Are we ready to forgive others for any harm that they have done to us, or are we bearing a grudge and looking for revenge?

Pause

Celebrant/service leader

Jesus asked us to be generous in offering forgiveness to others, just as God is generous in forgiving us. In the 'Our Father' we ask God to forgive us, just as we forgive others who harm us. Let us now say that prayer slowly together; look out for the words about forgiveness:

Our Father . . .

Order of Service 4

Opening hymn	*I, the Lord of sea and sky*	HON 186 LITON 376 PS 204

Introduction

Why we are gathered.

Prayer

Lord God, Lord of creation,
you have made us to love and serve you,
but we have turned our backs upon you,
and, so often, gone away from you.
May we use this opportunity
to return to you, our loving Father,
and to a renewed love for you. Amen.

Drama

Return to the Father

Hymn	*Our God loves us* *(My God loves me)*	HON 275, verses 1, 2, 4 and 5 LITON 560 PS 300

Examination of conscience

Prayer(s) of contrition (sorrow for sin)

See prayers 1 and 2 on back of service sheet.
(Read together)

Hymn	*Father, I place into your hands*	HON 114 LITON 251 PS 137

Invitation

If you would like to receive the sacrament of God's forgiveness, please stay behind now to meet with one of the priests.

Return to the Father

Luke 15:11-31

Preparation Stick for elderly father. Suitcase with coins or paper money in.

Characters A narrator; Father; Two sons: Jethro and Samuel; Three servants (non-speaking); Voices off.

Narrator *(At microphone)* This is a story that Jesus told; it could have been based on something that really happened. Our play opens on a farm in Galilee, that's the fertile part of the Holy Land, at the time of Jesus.

Father *(Old man, leaning on a stick, addressing Jethro)* We've got to get that harvest in before the rains come.

Jethro OK, Dad. *(To servants)* Come on then, let's get moving!

Father Where's Samuel got to?

Jethro Mooning around as usual . . . he's useless around the place; he's a waste of space. *(Samuel suddenly arrives)*

Samuel I heard that!

Jethro Well, you are. You're never here when you're needed.

Samuel That's because I hate this place . . . I hate the farm . . . I hate you and I'd clear out if I could . . . *(pause, has idea)* I could if I had the money.

Jethro Good riddance! We'd be better off without you!

Father Stop that, Jethro . . . that's not true . . . you are both my sons and you're both important to me.

Samuel Dad . . . you know you said that I could have half the value of the farm some day?

Father Yes *(hesitantly)* but that was after I'm no longer here . . . not now.

Jethro You can't do that! It would ruin us . . . half the farm! You don't do anything round here, why should you get half the farm?

Samuel *(Becoming aggressive)* Well, *(addressing his father)* you *promised* and I want it NOW.

Father Wait until after the harvest . . .

Samuel *(Interrupting)* NOW, NOW, NOW . . . I want it NOW. I'm going anyway. Do you want me to go around telling everyone how mean you are?

Father I can't sell the farm now . . . but you can have all my savings which is the same as half the value of the farm.

(Eldest son, Jethro, walks off in disgust. Father goes to get a suitcase of cash.)

Samuel *(Walking up and down)* Yes, got it. I'll go to the city . . . have a great time . . . make loads of friends and spend, spend, spend . . .

(Father returns and sadly hands over the suitcase. Samuel opens it with glee and starts counting . . .)

Father Don't you even trust me? You don't have to count it. That's all my savings – £65,000. Are you happy now?

Samuel Right, I'm off.

(He goes down the centre aisle, giving out notes 'Be my friend', 'Have a drink on me'. Father slumps down into a chair, head in hands.)

Narrator Samuel, the young son, travels far away to a city called Sychcopolis. There he books into an expensive hotel, buys the best of everything and has wild parties every night. *(Voices off, partying)* Meanwhile, back home, his old dad is grieving for his lost son. Every day he looks out, down the road to the farm, hoping desperately for his son to return. Months pass and he never shows.

In the city Samuel's money runs out. He gets thrown out of the hotel . . .

Voice off Get out of here! I'm not interested in your problems!

Narrator . . . and banned from the gambling casinos, the restaurants *(voices off)* and he has nothing left.

Voice off Tough! No money, no credit. Get a job.

Voice off Sorry, no work here. *(Repeated)*

Narrator The only job this Jewish boy could get was swilling out the pig pens.

Voice off Yuk! And double yuk!

Voice off A good Jewish boy looking after pigs . . . wow, what would his dad have to say about that!

Narrator Samuel smells . . . he's hungry . . . he's filthy . . . he's so miserable that he considers suicide. Then he thinks, 'I could at least be a servant on my dad's farm – not a son, of course, but I could look after the animals and get something to eat'.

Back home, his dad is still looking out for him. *(Action by Father)*
So smelly, filthy Samuel sets off home . . . *(He comes into view, dragging his feet, down the centre aisle. His father sees him . . . gets animated, calls for a servant and starts to go to meet his son. They meet in centre of the hall or church.)*

Father Samuel, Samuel, it is so wonderful to see you! *(Hugs him)*

Samuel Dad, I'm not fit or worthy to be your son. Let me be a servant . . .

Father Rubbish! You're my son! Welcome, welcome home! I've missed you so much. *(To hovering servants)* Quick, you, go and run him a bath. You, go and get those new clothes I bought. You, go and kill a calf. We are going to have party!

Narrator Jethro, the eldest son, is out on the far side of the farm when his brother returns. He knows nothing about it until, in the evening, he comes up to the farm house and hears the music, the laughter . . . He calls to a servant . . .

Jethro What's going on? Have we won the National Lottery?

Servant No, your brother's back and your dad's throwing a party!

Jethro I can't believe it! Has the old man gone mad? That brother of mine cleaned us out . . . took everything. How dare he show his face round here! Tell my father I won't come in until he throws him out! Got that?

Narrator The father leaves the party and comes out to reason with his son.

Father Jethro, come in, come in. Your brother's back.

Jethro Are you crazy? Mad? I'll never speak to him again. I've been with you, worked this farm for you. You've never once thrown a party for me and my friends.

Father Son, it's your *brother* returned. *My son* is back. I thought I would never see him again. I believed that he was dead. But he's alive; he's back. *Please,* for my sake, come in to the party and accept your brother.

Narrator And the story ends there! Did Jethro forgive his brother and accept him back? Did Samuel settle down to life on the farm? One thing is certain, the father's love was so great he could forgive all the bad things Samuel had done and treat him once again as a son.

Examination of Conscience
following the play *Return to the Father*

Celebrant/service leader

We have just seen enacted one of the best stories Jesus ever told. I'm sure you know that the father in the story represents God, our loving Father. The younger or the older son represents us. Let's look into our hearts and minds now to see if, like the younger son, we need to return to our Father and say 'sorry' for our wrong-doing.

Reader A

The young man asks for his inheritance. He goes to his dad and insults him by asking for the money he will get when his dad dies. Can you imagine that? But are we any better? We do insulting things sometimes and say spiteful and cruel things to our parents. Let's think of the times when we have been rude and disrespectful.

Pause

Reader B

The lad goes off and wastes all his money. The money that his father had earned and saved over the years. Our parents or guardians work hard and then generously give us money which we often waste on things that we don't really need. How generous are we in giving money to the poor? In helping aid agencies, like CAFOD, and other good causes?

Pause

Reader A

The lost son finds a job. The only job he can get is looking after pigs and he doesn't have enough to eat. Do we work hard and make a real effort to develop our gifts and talents? Do we waste food? Do we leave waste paper and rubbish around? Do we expect others to clear up after us? Do we care for the environment?

Pause

Reader B

The young man comes to his senses. He says to himself, 'I will return to my father.' Relationships are very important. Do we cherish our relationship with our family, our parents and brothers and sisters? Or do we fight with them and make no effort to be kind and helpful? What about relationships with our friends and the people in our form?

Pause

Reader A

The lost son returns home. His father is looking out for him and lovingly welcomes him. Do we love God, who looks out for us? Do we speak regularly to our Father in prayer? Do we go to Mass on Sundays? Do we turn to God when we have done wrong and ask for his forgiveness?

Pause

Reader B

The elder son will not enter the house. The elder son refuses to join the celebrations. He is jealous. Are we ever jealous and resentful of others? Are we unwilling to try to forgive others for what they have done to us? Do we refuse to mix with some people, thinking that we are better than them? Have we forgotten that Jesus asks us to love and care for everyone?

Pause

Celebrant/service leader

We have thought of a few things that we might have done wrong. There may be others. Let's be quiet for a few moments and think of any other sins that we want to tell God we are sorry for.

Order of Service 5

Opening hymn	*O Lord, my God*	HON 311, verses 1 and 3 LITON 529 PS 291
Introduction	Why we are gathered.	
Prayer	Almighty God, you are the king of the universe. All power and might comes from you. Whether we are famous or unknown, we all belong to you; and we all sin. May we take this opportunity of seeking your forgiveness and be reconciled with one another. Amen	
Drama	*The King Who Sinned*	
Hymn	*Amazing grace*	HON 31 LITON 131 PS 70
Examination of conscience		
Prayer(s) of contrition (sorrow for sin)	See prayers 1 and 2 on back of service sheet. *(Read together)*	
Hymn	*God forgave my sin*	HON 145 LITON 286 PS 157
Invitation	If you would like to receive the sacrament of God's forgiveness, please stay behind now to meet with one of the priests.	

The King Who Sinned

2 Samuel 11:1-17, 26-27; 12:1-9, 13

Preparations A simple gold crown, a regal looking chair (throne), a staff for Nathan.

Characters King David; Bathsheba; Joab; Uriah; Nathan; Zilah; Assorted soldiers and servants.

Narrator *(At microphone)* This story comes from the Old Testament and took place about 1,000 years before Jesus was born; so 3,000 years ago. It concerns the great King David, who, when the events take place, is rich and powerful and, according to the customs of that time, already has several wives. You need to remember that houses at that time had flat roofs where people often had their meals, slept at night or did other domestic jobs. The palace, being higher than other buildings, overlooked the neighbouring property. *(Pause)*

When the story begins David's armies are at war and besieging a town called Rabbah. On a warm evening in late spring David cannot sleep and wanders out onto the flat roof outside his bedroom.

(David wanders aimlessly on to a raised area or an area marked out by benches etc. He looks one way, then another . . . finally he stops, looks, draws back and returns to look more intently . . . looks round to make sure no one is watching . . . whistles softly. He steps back, looks once more, then wanders back the way he has come.)

Narrator What David had seen and then spied on was a young woman taking a bath on the roof-top of her house.

(The chair is put out and David comes in with two servants; they stand either side of the throne while David sits.)

David *(To one of the servants)* Zilah, you're a local man, aren't you? You know the people who live in the houses close to the palace.

Zilah Some, Your Highness, but not every one.

David I want you to find out who lives in the two houses on the east side of the palace. Go now!

Zilah Yes, Lord. *(He goes to leave)*

David On your way through the outer courtyard, ask Joab, my general, to come up to report to me. *(Zilah leaves and David turns to the second servant)*

When Zilah returns I want you to go and find out for me what is happening in the Northern province. I have had no news for a week.

(Joab arrives, accompanied by a soldier. David and Joab walk apart and are deep in conversation. Zilah returns. Joab leaves.)

David So, Zilah, what news have you for me?

Zilah The house nearest to the palace in occupied by an old couple, Jonah and Elisabeth. They originally lived . . . *(David interrupts)*

David The other house?

Zilah That's the home of Uriah the Hittite, who serves in your army – one of Joab's best soldiers. He's away at present with the army. There's just his young wife, Bathsheba, there at present, with a few women servants.

David *(Almost to himself)* Bathsheba . . . thank you, Zilah.

(All leave stage or area.)

Narrator David arranged for Bathsheba to come to the palace that evening, and she came secretly on many evenings, and stayed until early in the morning. Some weeks passed and one evening Bathsheba had some news for David.

(David and Bathsheba wander on to stage area. David has his arm around Bathsheba.)

David What's the matter? You've been so quiet.

Bathsheba I don't know how to tell you . . . *(pause)* . . . I'm pregnant . . . I'm going to have a baby.

(David breaks away from her.)

David You are quite sure . . . there's no mistake?

Bathsheba What can we do? If anyone finds out I'll be stoned to death.

David No, you won't. No one will find out. I'll arrange everything.

(They walk off together. Throne is put out. David comes in with the two servants.)

David Zilah, I want you to send a message to Joab at the siege of Rabbah and tell him to send Uriah the Hittite home. I want him to report to me personally.

(Zilah leaves and David and servant freeze.)

Narrator David's plan to get Uriah home and back with his wife, to cover up what had been going on, failed. Uriah came to see David, but did not go to see his wife. He stayed with the soldiers at the barracks and then returned to the army. David was desperate now and had another plan.

David *(To Zilah, who is entering)* Did you get in touch with Joab, my general?

Zilah Yes, Your Majesty, he's just coming.

(Joab enters)

David *(To the two servants)* Go! I want to speak to Joab on his own.

Joab Highness, you will be pleased to know all is going well at Rabbah. We have broken through the wall in three places and will storm the city at dawn the day after tomorrow, as soon as I return.

David That's excellent news . . . well done! I have a personal favour to ask. But before I do, I want to make it quite clear that I expect your complete loyalty and your silence. This conversation never took place. Is that clear?

Joab Of course, Your Majesty. I am your obedient servant.

David Uriah, the Hittite . . . I want you to put him in the front of the first wave of soldiers who will storm the wall at Rabbah. I don't expect him to survive . . . you understand my meaning.

Joab Someone has got to lead the attack. It might as well be him. I will take care of it, Your Highness.

David I will not forget your service to me in this.

(Joab bows low and leaves. David sits looking serious.)

Narrator David's plan succeeds. Uriah leads the attack on the town and is killed. After a reasonable time for mourning David took Bathsheba into his house and she became another of his wives. She gave birth to a baby boy. God, however, was not pleased with the way David had behaved and sent the prophet Nathan to challenge the King.

(The two servants come in and stand either side of the throne. Nathan, staff in hand, is escorted into the presence of King David. The servants have bowed but Nathan does not.)

Nathan I am the prophet Nathan, the voice of the Lord God.

David *(Scornfully)* I know very well who you are. What do you want, prophet?

Nathan I have a story for you. There were two men in the same town, one rich and one poor. The rich farmer had large flocks of sheep and cattle. The poor man had only one little lamb. It was the pet of the family; the poor man's children loved it, gave it a name and played with it.

The rich man had a visitor from a distant land and he wanted to impress him with a slap-up meal, so he sent his men to the poor man's house. They took the lamb, brought it to the rich man's farm, where it was killed for the meal.

Narrator The king was so angry he could hardly speak at first, then he shouted . . .

David That man must die! Death would be too good for him!

Nathan You are that man! This is what the Lord God has to say: 'I gave you everything, and you have repaid me with evil. You had Uriah killed so that you could take his wife.'

David I have sinned. I have done wrong. Will God forgive me?

Nathan If you publicly do penance and really repent.

(All actors freeze while narrator concludes; then all leave.)

Narrator David was truly sorry, once he had recognised his sin. He fasted and did penance for many days.

Later, David wrote poems and hymns called psalms. One of the best known is Psalm 50. The opening lines are these:
'Have mercy on me, O God,
according to your unfailing love;
according to your great compassion
blot out my sins.'

Examination of Conscience

following the play *The King Who Sinned*

Celebrant/service leader

Even kings and queens and famous people sin. In our dramatic presentation of the dreadful things that King David did, we saw how he deceived himself. He only realised what a terrible sin he had committed when the prophet Nathan came to confront him. Let's admit that we commit sins, and confront ourselves now, as we examine our consciences.

Reader A

David spied on a young woman. Have we spied on anyone or pried into other people's private lives, not respecting another's privacy? Are we secretive and underhand in our dealings with people? Are we open and honest with everyone?

Pause

Reader B

Bathsheba was unfaithful to her husband. Are we faithful and loyal to our friends? Do we keep our word once we've given it? Do we let our parents and guardians down by our behaviour? Do we remember the Christian teaching that the place for intimate sexual behaviour is within marriage?

Pause

Reader A

David's plan to get Uriah to visit his wife fails. Do we plot and plan to hurt others? Have we said or done anything that has caused hurt to another person? Have we bullied anyone by what we've done or said? Do we always tell the truth?

Pause

Reader B

David took Bathsheba as his wife. Do we take things that don't belong to us? Do we respect others' property? Do we return CDs, magazines, books, clothes and other things that we borrow from friends? Do we care for our homes and our school by not dropping rubbish and litter about?

Pause

Reader A

God was not pleased with David and sent his prophet. Do we listen to, and give respect to, the people God has given us as parents, guardians and teachers? Do we talk to God in prayer? Do we respect God by spending time with him?

Pause

Reader B

God said, 'I gave you everything and you repaid me with evil.' Are we grateful for all the gifts God has given us? For the gifts of life; good health; family and friends and so much more? Do you show your love and gratitude to your parents or guardians for what they do for you? Do we show our gratitude by helping at home?

Pause

Celebrant/service leader

King David realised how badly he had behaved and pleaded with God to forgive him. Now let us quietly think of anything else that we know we have done which needs God's forgiveness. Let us accept that it is our own fault; we alone are responsible and we need God to forgive us, as he forgave David.

Order of Service 6

Opening hymn	*Amazing grace*	HON 31 LITON 131 PS 70

Introduction

Why we are gathered.

Prayer

Almighty Father,
you know us better than we know ourselves.
You know that it is hard for us to admit
that we have hurt you and others,
and done wrong.
Give us your amazing grace;
open our eyes to our faults and our failures,
that we may humbly ask your forgiveness
and be reconciled with one another. Amen

Drama

The Weeping Sinner

Hymn	*Lay your hands gently upon us*	HON 225 LITON 413 PS 227

Examination of conscience

Prayer(s) of contrition (sorrow for sin)

See prayers 1 and 2 on back of service sheet
(Read together)

Hymn	*I will sing, I will sing*	HON 90, verses 1-4 LITON 385 PS 210

Invitation

If you would like to receive the sacrament of God's forgiveness, please stay behind now to meet with one of the priests.

The Weeping Sinner

Luke 7:36-50

Preparation A table and five chairs; a flagon-type vase or jar; a bottle of cheap, strong-smelling perfume; a wig with long hair (unless the 'girl' naturally has long hair).

Characters Jesus; a 'worldly' looking girl; Simon the Pharisee; three other Pharisees; servant.

Narrator In Jesus' day, if you were invited out to dinner, it was the custom to be offered an opportunity to wash and smarten yourself up before the meal, because the roads and streets were so dirty and dusty. On this occasion Jesus was invited out but not given the chance to 'freshen-up'.

(Jesus appears left of the table and chairs set out centre. Simon, standing at the table talking to the other three Pharisees, sees Jesus and goes to meet him.)

Simon Thank you for coming to my humble house. Come and meet my other guests.

(They proceed to the table, all shake hands and sit down. Conversation continues meanwhile.)

Pharisee 1 I'm glad to meet you – we've all heard so much about you.

Pharisee 2 You're from Galilee, aren't you?

Jesus Yes, I'm better known there. I don't often come up to Jerusalem.

Simon While we're waiting for the food, perhaps you can tell us why you are in Jerusalem.

(Big disturbance off-stage. Servant appears trying to stop young woman getting past him. She succeeds and heads for Jesus. She kneels at his feet.)

Simon *(Getting to his feet and addressing the servant)* Get this woman out of here.

Jesus Simon, please leave her. She's doing no harm.

(Simon sits down disgruntled. Servant leaves, reappears with tray of dishes; goes to serve the guests. Woman at Jesus' feet with back to audience.)

Pharisee 1 *(To Pharisee 2)* If he knew who this woman was he would never allow her near him.

Pharisee 2 *(To Pharisee 1)* It's a disgrace, a woman like that mixing with religious folk. *(Aside)* Simon should have her thrown out.

(The woman's crying can be heard. She gets up, opens the jar/vase and pours something (pretend) on the head of Jesus. The smell of perfume can be released at this point.)

Simon This really is too much! What on earth is she doing now?

Jesus Simon, I've got something to ask you.

Simon Well, I'm listening!

Jesus I've got a question for you. There were two people who were in debt. They both owed money to the same moneylender. The first owed £10,000, the second owed £1,000. They were unable to repay the money, so the moneylender let them both off – nothing to re-pay. Which of the two people will love the moneylender more?

Simon Well, I suppose it's obvious. The one who was let off the most.

Jesus Exactly. *(Turning to the woman, who is back on her knees)* You see this woman – I came into your house and you showed me no love and respect. You did not even offer me water to freshen-up. She has washed my feet with her tears of sorrow for what she has done. You gave me no greeting – she has kissed my feet and poured perfume on my head. She has shown much love – you showed little. She has done some dreadful things in her life, but she is deeply sorry. Her sins have been forgiven because she has shown such love. Someone like you, who is forgiven little, shows little love.

Pharisee 1 *(To Pharisee 2)* Who is this man who even forgives sins?

Jesus *(To the woman)* Go now. Go in peace, your faith has saved you.

Examination of Conscience

following the play *The Weeping Sinner*

Celebrant/service leader

In the play we saw how the religious leader, Simon the Pharisee, did not show courtesy and respect to his dinner guest, Jesus. It was the sinner who barged into the house who showed Jesus respect and love. This woman humbly accepted that she had sinned and looked for forgiveness.

Reader A

Simon invites Jesus to his home. Do we invite Jesus into our lives? Do we look for opportunities to talk to him in prayer? Do we pray regularly? Do we gather with the other friends of Jesus on a Sunday to celebrate the Eucharist (Mass) with them? Are we generous in inviting friends to our home for time together?

Pause

Reader B

Simon orders: 'Get this woman out of here.' Have we remembered and tried to live by the words of Jesus, that we should love one another? Do we ever act in a bullying way? Have we hurt anyone by cruel remarks or comments? Have you been a good friend? Have you cut out or excluded any one in your form? Have you been prejudiced against anyone?

Pause

Reader A

Simon replied to Jesus, 'Well, I'm listening.' Are we ever insolent and rude at home, causing hurt to those who love us? Are we insolent and rude at school to teachers and other members of staff? Do we respond with respect to those who ask us to help or do things? Do we offer to help at home or duck out of the way and make excuses?

Pause

Reader B

'The first owed £10,000 pounds, the second owed £1,000.' Have we borrowed things and not returned them? Do you owe money to anyone and have not made an effort to repay it? Have you stolen anything? Are we really honest and trustworthy?

Pause

Reader A

Jesus said, 'Her sins have been forgiven because she has shown much love.' Are we ready to forgive others, as Jesus asks? Or are we harbouring resentment, unwilling to forgive? Do we feel like getting back at someone for what they have done to us? Are we all genuine and sincere about saying 'sorry' for the bad things we've done?

Pause

Celebrant/service leader

To receive God's forgiveness we must be prepared to try hard to forgive others. There can be no thoughts of revenge or getting back at anyone, if we are to be forgiven ourselves. Let's be quiet for a few minutes and in the silence ask ourselves if there is anything else we need to seek God's forgiveness for.

Order of Service 7

Opening hymn	*Lord Jesus Christ*	HON 247 LITON 447 PS 247
Introduction	Why we are gathered.	

Prayer

Heavenly Father,
your Son told us not to judge others
if we do not want to be judged by you;
but we have and we do judge others.
May we honestly and sincerely open our hearts to you now,
accept that we have done wrong,
seek your forgiveness
and be assured of your love. Amen.

Drama	*The Condemned Woman*	
Hymn	*Look around you*	HON 241 LITON 440 PS 244
Examination of conscience		
Prayer(s) of contrition (sorrow for sin)	See prayers 1 and 2 on back of service sheet *(Read together)*	
Hymn	*Make me a channel of your peace*	HON 262 LITON 470 PS 263

Invitation

If you would like to receive the sacrament of God's forgiveness, please stay behind now to meet with one of the priests.

The Condemned Woman

John 8:1-11

Preparations Twenty/thirty large balls made of crumpled newspaper. Because Jesus remains seated throughout the play, he needs to be on a raised area of some kind to be clearly visible.

Characters Jesus; a group of five or six disciples (only one speaks); Pharisee 1; Pharisee 2; a crowd of seven or eight; the young woman.

Narrator *(At a microphone)* The Jewish Law was very strictly kept at the time of Jesus. In the Book of Leviticus it clearly states that any person, male or female, caught committing adultery (that is, being unfaithful to a married partner) should be stoned to death. On this occasion, recorded in John's Gospel, the man involved appears to have escaped.

Jesus was quietly teaching a group of his followers when a crowd interrupted.

(Jesus is sitting on the ground, to the left, with his disciples)

Disciple The Scriptures tell us to love God. What is new about what you are telling us?

Jesus I am telling you that God wants our love but he also wants us to love others – enemies as well as friends.

(Crowd interrupts, entering noisily from the right. The two Pharisees are dragging a young woman, who is struggling. They throw her down in front of Jesus.)

Pharisee 1 Here you are, rabbi! Here's a problem for you.

Pharisee 2 Yes, you teach love. What have you got to say about this sinner?

Pharisee 1 Moses teaches us, in our Holy Scriptures, that a woman like this who is caught committing adultery should be stoned to death.

Crowd *(Picking up the 'stones' littered around the place)* Yes, yes, stoned to death.

Pharisee 2 *(Addressing Jesus)* What have you got to say?

(Jesus ignores the speaker and bends down to write in the dust.)

Narrator This is not what it seems. It is a very clever trap for Jesus. If Jesus says, 'Stone her' his disciples will think him a hypocrite. How can

Jesus say 'Love one another' one minute and then say it is alright to stone a woman to death? On the other hand, if he says, 'Let her go', the Pharisees will accuse him of encouraging them to break the Law of Moses and no good Jew could do that. Moreover, Jesus might find himself being stoned for even suggesting it! Jesus cleverly avoids the trap.

(The disciples with Jesus withdraw behind him, leaving Jesus alone facing the crowd.)

Pharisee 1 *(Irritated by Jesus' silence)* Have you no answer? What are we to do with this sinner?

Pharisee 2 Shall we stone her?

(The woman stands up.)

Jesus *(Looking up)* If anyone of you is without sin, let him be the first to throw a stone at her.

(Jesus bends down to continue writing in the dust. There is silence; first the crowd look at one another, then at the ground and gradually, one by one, they put their 'stones' down and slip quietly away. The two Pharisees are the last to leave.)

Jesus *(Looking up and addressing the woman standing before him)* Where are your accusers? Has no one condemned you?

Woman No one, Sir.

Jesus Then neither do I condemn you. Go now and do not sin again.

(The woman hurries away. The disciples gather round Jesus and start chattering; Jesus stands and all depart.)

Examination of Conscience

following the play *The Condemned Woman*

Celebrant/service leader

We saw an actual event in the life of Jesus enacted in our play. Jesus saved the life of the woman who had sinned by helping the people in the crowd to realise that they too were sinners and had no right to judge and condemn the woman. Let us now look into our own hearts and minds, and accept that we too commit sin.

Reader A

Jesus speaks of loving God and our neighbour. Do we take the words of Jesus seriously? Do we really try to love God and show him our love by speaking to him in prayer and going to the Eucharist on a Sunday? 'Our neighbour' includes the people we don't like in our form – are we really trying to show them respect and care for them?

Pause

Reader B

The crowd drag a woman who has sinned before Jesus. The crowd want to humiliate the woman. Do we make fun of people and try to make them look small and humiliate them? Do we spread stories about people, destroying their good names? Do we look down on anyone and think that we are superior and better than them?

Pause

Reader A

'Shall we stone her?' the Pharisees ask. Do we use violence: violent words or actions? Have we bullied anyone or made someone's life miserable by what we have done or said? Have we picked on a brother or sister, and made their lives unhappy? Have you been a good and loyal friend? Have you been kind to animals?

Pause

Reader B

Jesus says that the person who has not sinned may throw the first stone. Are we proud and full of ourselves, refusing to believe that we sin and do wrong? Do we maturely accept responsibility for our wrongdoing? Do we humbly ask forgiveness? Are we ready to forgive others for what they may have done to us?

Pause

Reader A

Jesus says to the woman, 'Go and do not sin again.' The woman believes in the authority of Jesus and goes home. Do we respect the authority of our parents or guardians? Do we ever try to deceive them and tell them lies? Do we respect the authority of our teachers? Do we respect ourselves, our bodies and our health?

Pause

Celebrant/service leader

Let us sit quietly for a few moments, thinking of any other wrong things that we may have done. Let us remember the last few words of Jesus, 'Go and do not sin again'. No matter what we may have done, God, our loving Father, will always forgive us if we really are sorry and mean to try never to do it again.

Order of Service 8

Opening hymn	*Walk with me*	HON 441, verses 1-4 LITON 706 PS 371

Introduction

Why we are gathered.

Prayer

Loving Father,
throughout the whole of human history
you have been a faithful God.
We have been repeatedly unfaithful to you,
and to one another.
May we use this opportunity
to renew our love for you
and our faithfulness. Amen.

Drama

Peter Disowns Jesus

Hymn	*Do not be afraid*	HON 109 LITON 240 PS 129

Examination of conscience

Prayers of contrition (sorrow for sin)

See prayers 1 and 2 on back of sheet.
(Read together)

Hymn	*Peace, perfect peace*	HON 343, verses 1, 2 and 5 LITON 574 PS 304

Invitation

If you would like to receive the sacrament of God's forgiveness, please stay behind now to meet with one of the priests.

Peter Disowns Jesus

Mark 14:66-72

Preparations If possible a 'campfire' made of wood and red crepe paper. Two staves or long sticks for the guards.

Characters Narrator; two readers; Peter; two servant women; group of other servants (at least four); two guards; Jesus (non-speaking part).

(Narrator needs to stand apart from the action at a microphone.)

Narrator Jesus and his friends spent a happy evening celebrating the Jewish festival of Passover, enjoying a special meal with prayers and hymns. At the end of the meal Jesus became very quiet and serious. He said:

Reader A One of you is about to betray me.

Narrator The mood of the evening suddenly changed. There was a stunned silence; then Peter spoke up:

Reader B I'd never betray you, Lord. Even if all these betrayed you, I wouldn't.

Narrator Jesus looked round the group and said:

Reader A You will all fall away.

Narrator In the silence Peter again protested:

Reader B Even if I have to die for you, I will never let you down.

Narrator After a moment of silence Jesus replied:

Reader A I'm telling you the truth. Today, yes, tonight, before the cock crows heralding the dawn, you will disown me. Not once, but three times.

Narrator Peter interrupted:

Reader B No, Lord, you've got that wrong. I will never betray you.

Narrator All the others said the same. A few minutes later they sang their closing hymn and left for the Garden of Gethsemane, where Jesus wanted to spend some time alone. *(Long pause)* While in the Garden, Jesus was arrested by the Temple guards, who found him there. All his friends ran away in the dark. Only Peter stayed, in the dark, following the crowd who had arrested Jesus right into the courtyard of the High Priest's house.

(Actors move into place. Servants sit and stand round a 'campfire'. The two guards stand, with their staves, at some distance to the right.)

First servant woman It's a cold night, it's as well someone lit the fire.

Second servant woman How long are they going to be? It's not right being dragged out of your bed at this hour. What's so important that it can't keep to the morning?

Servant 1 It's that prophet from Galilee. The Council's trying him.

Second servant woman What for? What's he done that we've got to get out of bed and come here in the middle of the night?

First servant woman Must be bad to bring the Council out at this time of night.

(Peter drifts into the scene from the left and stands near the first woman, warming himself at the fire.)

Servant 2 I heard that they've been trying to get him for months.

First servant woman *(Looking more closely at Peter)* I've seen you before . . . you're one of the prophet's followers. You were with that Jesus.

Peter *(Drawing back)* No. I don't know what you're talking about.

(Peter moves round to the other side of the fire; but the second servant woman follows him.)

Second servant woman Yes, you are. You are one of them.

Peter I'm not. I've told you I'm not. Leave me alone. I don't know the man.

(The two guards leave.)

Narrator A little time passed and Peter was beginning to feel safer when suddenly one of the crowd around the fire said, pointing at him:

Servant 3 I've been watching you. You are one of those followers of Jesus.

Peter I'm not.

Servant 4 There you are! Even your voice betrays you. You're from Galilee.

Peter I don't know this man Jesus. I swear to you that I know nothing about him. I've never even met him.

(The two guards reappear with Jesus between them. They are holding the arms of Jesus, with their staves in their right and left hands respectively. They pass behind the scene. Jesus looks up at Peter as he passes. Their eyes meet. Nothing is said.)

Narrator At that moment the cock crowed for the second time. *(Do* not *provide the sound. It may cause laughter and break the atmosphere.)*

(Peter looks startled.)

Narrator Peter remembered what Jesus had said: 'Before the cock crows twice you will have disowned me three times.' He left, weeping bitterly.

(Peter leaves, shoulders hunched. After a slight pause all leave.)

Examination of Conscience

following the play *Peter Disowns Jesus*

Celebrant/service leader

What a story! Peter boasted that he would stick by Jesus but when the moment came, he lost all his courage *(if preferred 'he bottled out')* and denied that he even knew Jesus. A shameful story; but what would we have done in the same situation? Don't we say that we are Christians – friends of Jesus – but then let him down? Let's think about that for a few minutes.

Reader A

Peter boasted, 'I will never let you down.' Have we made promises to be loyal to Jesus? *(If appropriate 'Have you made a commitment at your confirmation? Are you living up to it?')* Do we speak to our friend, Jesus, regularly in prayer? Do we join with his other friends for Mass on Sunday? Have we been loyal to our own friends? Are you a 'show-off', going around boasting about what you have and what you've done?

Pause

Reader B

Jesus said, 'I'm telling you the truth.' Do we always tell the truth? Can our parents or guardians trust what we tell them? Are we ever underhand or deceitful? Can people trust us with personal confidences or do we spread gossip about others? Are we trust-worthy? Have we taken anything that does not belong to us?

Pause

Reader A

All his friends ran away in the dark. Do we 'clear off' and leave others alone to tidy up or put things away? Do we drop litter and expect other people to come along and clear up after us? Do we selfishly leave our parents or guardians to do everything in the home? Do we remember that Jesus asks us to love one another, and that means offering to help others?

Pause

Reader B

Peter said, 'I swear to you that I don't even know the man.' Are we proud or ashamed to be Christians – friends of Jesus? When you are out with your friends *(mates)* do you deny being a Christian? Do you pretend that you don't know him? Are we really grateful for the gift of faith or just embarrassed to belong to the Church?

Pause

Reader A

Peter left, weeping bitterly. If we are really sorry about how we have treated our friend Jesus, are we really going to try to be a better friend and do what he asks? Are we ready to forgive every-one – that is *everyone*, not just our friends – for what they may have done to us? God only forgives us if we are prepared and willing to forgive others.

Pause

Celebrant/service leader

The good news is that Peter was really very sorry for what he did; and Jesus forgave him. We have some serious thoughts to spend a few quiet moments on now. Let's sit in silence and try to think of any other things that we know we have done wrong. Then we shall tell God how we are ready to forgive others and ask his forgiveness.

Prayers

Prayers of sorrow

1. O my God,
   because you are so good to me,
   I am very sorry that I have sinned against you.
   With your help I will not sin again. Amen.

2. Lord God, our loving Father,
   you know all my weaknesses and failures.
   I come to you with real sorrow in my heart.
   Forgive me, accept me, strengthen me. Amen.

Prayers of discipleship

3. Day by day,
   O dear Lord,
   three things I pray:
   to see you more clearly,
   love you more dearly,
   follow you more nearly,
   day by day. Amen.

4. Teach us, good Lord,
   to serve you as you deserve;
   to give and not to count the cost;
   to fight and not to heed the wounds;
   to toil and not to seek for rest;
   to labour and to ask for no reward,
   save that of knowing that we do your will;
   through Jesus Christ our Lord. Amen.

Return to the Father

Our making-up service for Lent

Order of service

(see pages 11, 17, 23, 29, 35, 43, 49 and 55)

THE SACRAMENT OF FORGIVENESS

Making up with God and one another

What to do

First, and most important, do not worry.

The priest is there to help you . . .

You cannot make a mistake, as long as you share with him:

- what is making you anxious
- anything you would like to talk about.

Remember, you are seeing the priest so that he can help you make up with God and people you may have hurt.

Three things are necessary:

- the priest needs to know how long it is since you last spoke to a priest about your sins. Is it weeks or months or years?
- the priest will pass God's forgiveness on to you but first you need to tell him what you are sorry for.
- the priest will want to hear you say a prayer telling God you are sorry for what you have done. (You may like to use one of the prayers on the back of this sheet.)

Finally

Everything you tell the priest is kept in perfect secrecy; he cannot tell anyone what you have shared with him.

When you leave the priest, kneel for a few minutes in the church, quietly saying any prayers he has asked you to say. Don't forget to say 'thank you' to God for forgiving you.

Suggested Readings for Services of Reconciliation

It may not always be possible or appropriate to use plays or dramatised readings for a school service of reconciliation. Here is a short selection of readings to choose from for occasions when a reading from the Scriptures is required.

OLD TESTAMENT

Genesis 18:17-33

Abraham intercedes with God
'I will not destroy it,' he replied, 'for the sake of ten.'
This reading could easily be adapted for dramatised reading using three readers: a narrator, God and Abraham.

Exodus 20:1-21

The Ten Commandments
'I am Yahweh your God . . . you shall have no other gods to rival me.'
The words 'Do not be afraid' (verse 20) could be picked up and the reading followed by the hymn 'Do not be afraid'.

Deuteronomy 6:4-9

God's great commandment
'You must love Yahweh your God with all your strength.'
This could be taken with the New Testament reading, Mark 12:28-34.

Micah 6:1-9

Walk humbly with your God
While the last verse is beautiful and well known, the preceding verses will need an explanatory introduction.

NEW TESTAMENT: The Letters

Romans 5:6-11 *Christ died for us while we were still sinners*

Romans 13:8-14 *Love is the fulfilment of the Law*

Ephesians 2:1-6 *God brought us to live in Christ*

Ephesians 5:1-14 *Behave as children of light*

Hebrews 12:1-4 *Let us keep our eyes fixed on Jesus*

1 John 2:3-11 *Anyone who hates his brother is still in the dark*

NEW TESTAMENT: Gospel readings

Matthew 9:1-9	*The cure of a paralytic* 'Take comfort . . . your sins are forgiven.'
Matthew 9:10-13	*Jesus eats with sinners* 'I came to call not the upright, but sinners.'
Luke 15:1-7	*The lost sheep* 'There will be more rejoicing . . . over one sinner.'
John 15:1-8	*Branches of the Vine* 'Every branch that does not bear fruit . . .'
John 15:9-14	*The true friends of Christ* 'You are my friends if you do what I command you.'